UNDERSTANDING BITCOIN

The Step By Step Guide to Ownership

James Richards, M.B.A.

www.UnderstandingBitcoin.com

ISBN-10: 1981314431
ISBN-13: 978-1981314430

DEDICATION

To my mother who convinced me at a young age that I could do anything that I put my mind to, and my father for gifting me the ability to put a strategy and time frame around the goals I strive for...

CONTENTS

AUTHOR'S PREFACE

This book is for informational purposes only. I am not an investment advisor, a tax attorney, or a CPA, and this is not investment advice. The purpose of this book is only to get you familiar with the concepts surrounding Bitcoin, and guide you to some other places to begin your personal due diligence. Before making any investments you should consult your investment advisor, tax attorney, and CPA. If you do not understand this please go back and read again. Thank you in advance.

-   *James Richards*

1 AN ABRIDGED HISTORY OF MONEY

"Mo' Money, Mo' Problems"
- Puff Daddy

The problem in search of a solution was as follows. As humanity moved into an agrarian society, humans planted and harvested crops like rice, wheat, and corn with the seasons. To survive year round, they stored these calories for times when these crops were not in harvest.

As humans became proficient at this, they began to have excess calories from their efforts. This enabled other humans to specialize in other areas, like, for instance, making clothes. These extra calories, in the form of say rice, were then *"Bartered"* for clothes and visa versa.

It was not long after, that humans discovered, it could be hard to find the exact right person to *"Barter"* with, in the exact right amount, for all of the things that they needed. Who wants half a pair of pants? Enter Gold and Silver.

Gold and Silver had *"Seven Advantages"* as a *"Currency"* including:

1. <u>Divisibility</u> – Can be broken in half or quarters, etc.
2. <u>Store of Value</u> – Limited in Quantity.
3. <u>Durability</u> – Immutable.
4. <u>Uniformity</u> – One equal size piece is the same as another.
5. <u>Transportability</u> – Not too heavy in small amounts.
6. <u>Consensus of Acceptance</u> – Agreed to have value among many.
7. <u>Non-Counterfeitablity</u> – The Alchemists tried.

Rome once was a great empire and, as such, utilized pure Silver coins, called the *"Denarius"*, for trade throughout its lands. Because of the *"Seven Advantages"* above, this currency was widely accepted and drove commerce on a scale the world have never previously seen. Unfortunately, as many societies eventually do, they became overextended from wars, public works, and governance excesses, and needed a way to fund these great expenditures. They began to *"Debase the Currency"* by adding less precious metals like Copper and Lead to their coins and demanded that they still be accepted. Of course, this eventually ended in inflation, and hastened the demise of this once mighty empire, Rome. Sound familiar at all, in our modern world? I guess that is why they say *"Those that do not understand history are doomed to repeat it"*.

The Chinese are credited with the next major advance in currency as they took deposits of Gold and Silver into their Financial Institutions and gave *"Receipts"* for these deposits which were redeemable by the bearer upon request. The first *"Paper Money"*. It did not take long, post this advancement, for people to figure out that they could more conveniently, just exchange the *"Receipts"* instead of going to the bank and taking out, then putting back in, the Gold and Silver. This was actually the first *"Paper Money"* that was backed by Gold and Silver.

America adopted this model when it first printed its own money, post a bad break-up with Britain. Various different banks printed their own notes, and they were exchanged among its people. In 1913, a number of bankers decided that we needed a *"Central Bank"* (many great books have been written on this), and they created the *"Federal Reserve Bank"*, unconstitutionally I might add. Although it sounds like a government agency, it is actually a secret consortium of banks that control our money supply.

In 1933, the *"Federal Reserve Bank"*, in a further consolidation of power, through a Presidential *"Executive Order"*, demanded that all American Citizens turn over ALL of their Gold Bullion, Gold Coins, and Gold Certificates under the threat of monetary fines and up to 10 years in prison! The American Public complied.

In 1944, the post WWII Breton Woods Agreement was adopted, and the US Dollar became the sole, *"World Reserve Currency"*. As the US had over 17,000 tons of gold or approximately 64% of global gold reserves, this seemed like a reasonable solution to a stable reserve currency. To further aid acceptance globally, the US Dollar was fixed at a rate of $35.00 per ounce of gold, and we could go to a bank with $35.00 and get an ounce of gold. The US promised the world that we would maintain this pegged rate.

In 1971, for multiple reasons outside the scope of this book (wars, large domestic spending projects, government excesses, escalating debt, etc. – Ugh, sound familiar again) the President of the United States *"Temporarily Suspended the Coverability of the US Dollar to Gold"* and thereby, *"Debased the Global Reserve Currency"*. It is still *"Suspended"* to this day!

Now the *"World Reserve Currency"*, the US Dollar, was officially a *"Fiat Currency"* backed by the promise of the US Government to pay it back and, well, nothing else. So much for this former promise to the globe, I guess things change.

Not surprisingly, the world immediately began to experience inflation and, of course, devaluation of the US Dollar. What could the US do to increase demand for this failing *"Fiat Currency"*? Enter Saudi Arabia.

The US was able to *"convince"* Saudi Arabia that all oil should be settled in US Dollars globally only, and, presto, the *"PetroDollar"* was born. All oil globally was to trade in this *"World Reserve Currency"* (at times at gunpoint) which naturally created great demand for US Dollars and this system is still in use today…mostly.

In the late 1970s, interest rates were in the high teens due to *"Stagflation"* or high degrees of inflation without wage growth, due predominately to this abrupt switch to *"Fiat Currency"*. Since that time, we have seen a steady lowering of the interest rates to promote growth and employment. To date this has generally worked.

Unfortunately, post the *"The Great Recession"* we are at effectively 0% interest rates and some world governments have even gone to negative interest rates! The World has also started printing money like there is no tomorrow. Do they know something we do not? What happens during the next crisis? *Are we headed for the "Minsky Moment"? What would that look like in our modern world, and where would wealth migrate to?*

By the way, all *"Fiat Currencies"* in the history of the world have eventually gone to zero, except the US Dollar and its affiliates…So far. *Rot Roh Shaggy.*

2 CENTRALIZATION VS. DECENTRALIZATION

"I Know the Middleman, But He Don't Know Me"
- Gucci Main

"Bartering" was decentralized by its nature. We did not need to go through a bank or payment processor, we just agreed and did it. This was the original *"Peer to Peer"* exchange.

Gold and Silver were decentralized when they were utilized for exchange. Even when governments entered the picture and stamped out Gold and Silver coins, you could still melt them for their intrinsic value (still fairly decentralized even though the governments controlled the stamping).

Governments and Bankers, in their infinite wisdom, decided we needed safety or, maybe, they needed control. Enter *"Centralized Safety"*. First it was a safe place to store your Gold, Silver, and Dollars, then it was for a small fee, and now they have *"Full Custody"*. Since technically they now own these items, the fees have continued to compound. Now, they are telling you that you cannot get your cash or spend it in certain ways without permission (some of this is for very good reason but, you see the control creep here, for law abiding citizens like us).

Today, we continue to see further abuses of these powers (literally more everyday), including software that charges the largest daily charges first in your checking account, so that if you are short on funds, they can hit you with multiple overdraft charges, the opening of multiple accounts without your permission, or, in some cases, even worse. Were we not the taxpayers that recently bailed them out? They certainly are not acting like that! With all of the hubris, it is like they were daring a replacement to present itself. Well, *"Dare Accepted"*, and Bitcoin is *"Double-Dog Daring"* them back. Can we even imagine the US Dollar not being the *"Best House on a Bad Block"*, like it has been for so long? The world changes whether we are prepared or not.

3 BITCOIN IS BORN IN CHAOS – THE GREAT RECESSION

Fortunately for Humanity, in Our Darkest Moments, Hope Presents Itself.

- James Richards

In 2008, the bill was coming due for racking up massive debt, perilous derivatives, and utilizing the housing market as a casino for Bankers' edification (sadly, the bill always comes due). The US, and then the world at large, became victims of this *"Victimless Crime"* and we all had to look at ourselves in the mirror and reevaluate what we had let transpire. Furthermore, if we are honest, we had really become a party to this debt and derivative party (who doesn't like cheap money?).

We literally came within hours of the entire *"Global Monetary System"* melting down into nothingness. Fortunately the Federal Reserve came to the rescue. *"We are the government and we are here to help!"*, they said and actually did manage to save the system, for now. They accomplished this by opening up a potentially unlimited money supply, *"Fiat Money Supply"* that is. How wonderful for us all?

Shortly after the *"To Big to Fail"* consolidations, 0% interest rates, and other helicopter dumps of QE monies, the rest of the world caught on and, got in on the action. Not to be outdone, they went to *"Negative Interest Rates"* and started helicopter dropping QE money of their own. After all, China need infrastructure, and the Western Economies need to spend not save, as their GDPs are made up of 70% consumer spending. This spending cannot and will not stop, or something like that. But what about the abuse to the money and the monetary system? Is this a *"Free Lunch"*?

In October 2008, quietly, and to little fanfare, Satoshi Nakamoto released a *"White Paper"* onto the Internet called *"Bitcoin, A Peer-to-Peer Electronic Cash System"*. In January 2009, he then followed up by released onto the Internet, the software to operate the Network and the *"Bitcoin Cryptocurrency"* we now know as, **"Bitcoin"**. The inventor or inventors of Bitcoin quickly went underground from an identity perspective, due to the adoption of this currency and the threat it poses to global currencies (Wouldn't you?).

Since that time, his/her/their Bitcoins have become the *"Honey Badger of Money"* and are still growing in value to this day. No, I am not Satoshi Nakamoto and so far *"Bitcoins Don't Care"* what anyone says or does, they keep rising. Still today, they are the *"Honey Badger of Money"*, pretty much doing whatever they want, no matter what anyone else would prefer. Look it up *(Honey Badger Don't Care)* for a laugh on https://youtube.com. The comparisons are striking.

4 WORLD CURRENCIES SINCE THE GREAT RECESSION

"Look Like It's About to Rain... What a Shame...
...Against My Window...I Can't Stand the Rain"
-   Missy Elliot, Timberland, and Ann Peebles

Since the Great Recession, the US's debt has topped $20+ trillion (See Entitlements), China's has surpassed $40+ trillion (See Misallocation of Resources for Infrastructure), Japan is at $10+ trillion (See as a Population Inversion), and the EU, depending on what estimate you look at, is possibly in worse shape (See *"Cradle to Grave"* Progressive Societies). By the way, all of these have surpassed the *"Magic Debt-to-GDP Number"* of over 100% (Some substantially past, like Japan). Not good. Not good at all. Do we really think these debts will EVER be repaid?

Not to worry, we are now hearing *"Lower for Longer"* on rates, and *"The Pocketbook is Fully Open"*, and *"QE to Infinity"*, oh really? Does this make sense to anyone, or is it just me? But, they say, we have to get the US, and the World, spending again through confidence (or debt in reality). Can we?

Follow this sobering line of logic:

1. All economies are tethered in the world economy and, as we saw in the Great Recession, there is no escaping that.

2. The US economy is currently the largest economy in the world and, as the US goes, so does the world economy. The US is in a

precarious position, as it attempts to *"Raise Interest Rates and De-Lever the Fed's Balance Sheet, Simultaneously"*. Yes, we bought our own debt…wow, that one was really original!

3. Approximately 70% of the US economy is consumer spending.

4. Statistically, peak spending for an average US consumer is in their late 40s (Buy a big house, furnish this house, buy better cars, kids go to college, etc.)(See Harry Dent).

5. The Baby Boomer Demographic, which has shattered every *"US Lifestyle Paradigm"* as they have passed through it, has had major, mind bending, influences on the economy resulting from their sheer numbers (tons of great books on this).

6. On average, the Baby Boomers hit their late 40s in, you guessed it, the year of 2007. This is, I am sure just coincidently, the start of the Global Meltdown and following pursuant Great Recession.

7. Now, Boomers have stopped spending at these rates and are predominately thinking about saving for retirement. Unfortunately for them, the entire globe is *"Yield-Starved"* (Remember 0% interest rates). They began *"Saving for Retirement"* all at the same time, and the Global Economy is *"Feeling the Pinch"*.

8. Baby Boomers are done spending big and the following generation is not, nearly large enough to close the gap. This shift is triggering the *"D"* word – *"Deflation"*. *SEE JAPAN DURING THE PAST TWO DECADES, AS THE PERFECT CASE STUDY OF AN AGING POPULATION…HELLO?*

9. Our Government regularly says that we cannot have deflation because, no one will spend their money at the same rate. Something you would want to buy today will cost less tomorrow so you defer your purchase.

10. The US prints more even money to *"Inflate Us To Prosperity"* and will have to continue to do so to fund our *"Unfunded Liabilities"* (See Baby Boomer Social Security and Medicare Liabilities).

11. None of the above even includes the $4+ quadrillion in

derivatives currently out there. Yes, quadrillion with a *"Q"*. It might as well be spelled with a *"WTF"*.

12. If you have recently read the legal agreement associated with your bank accounts/financial accounts, most of them now placed your *"safe"* checking and savings deposit accounts in a subordinate position to the Bank's derivative risk (They are counting on you not reading them and clicking *"Accept"*, unfortunately, I did read them and am writing about it). Can you say *"Bail-In"* if it goes poorly? That means that most financial institutions have the right to take, say 20% of your money to save the bank because of their bad derivative bets! Next time, they will not even have to ask Congress for our money (See Cypress).

13. That is clearly not enough, so now, *"Let's Cut Taxes"*

14. Wealth sees what is coming, ***"Hyper-Inflation"***, and starts running for places to hide or *"Store Value"* {Real Estate in Global Cities (New York, San Francisco, Beijing, Sidney, London), Art, Classic Cars, Stocks, Commodities, Precious Metals, etc. – All at or near record levels, I might add}.

15. Smart Wealth slowly discovers Bitcoin, as a new *"Store of Wealth"*. Simultaneously, TRUST in our LEADERS and FINANCIAL INSTUTIONS denigrates further and further. Government Officials, Congressmen, Bankers, Businessmen, and other Institutional Leaders begin *"Retiring Early"* or *"Are Resigning Effective Immediately"* in unprecedented numbers before being outed for absolutely unacceptable behaviors. This will be our *"Tell"* and *"Signal Further Adoption"* of Bitcoin. After all, Bitcoin is a *"Crisis Currency"*, right?.

16. Bitcoin's price continues to rise as more and more wealth crowds in to this limited asset. Only 21,000,000 Bitcoins ever.

17. Rome, failed from it outermost *"Provinces"* inward, so watch Spain, Italy, Venezuela, etc. in the *"Dollar Empire"*. In these locations, we all will find the *"Canary in the Coal Mine"*.

Not a pretty picture, nor one I relish writing about, but, one we will not avoid. Sorry, there will not be a *"Hollywood Ending"* here, as much as we wish it would come. Furthermore, it will happen faster than we will be able to process. History has proven this too many times, actually, every time.

5 WHY BITCOIN?

"Hate it or Love it, the underdog's on Top"
-   The Game and 50 Cent

Unlike the U.S. Dollar and other World Currencies, there will only be 21 million Bitcoins ever, period, end of statement, and this is a *"Mathematical Certainty"*. When it is politically expedient, when it would really help the economy, or even when it would just plain be convenient, more Bitcoins will NOT be an option, and governments and banks cannot change this, EVER. What a perfect **"Store of Value"**, if we needed one, that is.

There is no Bitcoin CEO to influence, there is no Bitcoin Headquarters to raid, there is only a proven system of *"Open Source"* software that cannot be cracked, and that has been released into the thing called the *"Internet"* which, coincidently, the globe has become *"Critically Dependent Upon"*. Transactions on this system are *"Mined"* through *"Hashing"* which is a system that independently verifies every transaction, for a small fee, in a *"Decentralized Ledger"* manner (there is that dang word again). Bitcoins do not have the need for *"Intermediaries"* (aka Banks, Transaction Networks, or Governments) and, thereby, are a *"Disintermediary Force"* (kind of like when you go directly to the manufacture to buy a good and cut out the middleman…Think Amazon, AirBnB, and Uber…does anyone take a taxi, if they do not have to, anymore?). By the way, this is why Bankers are Bitcoins worse critics. Bitcoin adoption is potentially an *"Extinction Level Event"* for them if they cannot adapt to this new entrant/technology on the global scene. They will definitely attempt to compete through their Bank Branded *"Blockchain Products"*. Now, coming to a Financial Institution near you, XYZBankBlockCoins! If you can't beat them join them, I guess.

Do not be fooled, this is just another attempt to control your money through resurrection of their old systems. Bitcoin is *"Open Source"*, so anyone can build products that utilize the software and system. Theirs will undoubtedly be *"Proprietary"* (sad trombone…*"Whaaa Whaaaa"*). Bitcoin charges much lower fees than they charge…have you seen how much they charge a legal, migrant worker (say, picking fruit for a season) to send money back to their home country and family, like 7 to 8%! Bitcoin's transactions occur in minutes versus hours or days for the Bankers'. Sounds like the gig may be up boys! What a party it has been though.

How is all of this possible, you ask? Encryption is the key to loosening this strangle hold around the globe's neck. Every transaction that is done essentially morphs into another that is private to the new holder. It is also impossible to work backwards and undoing the Blockchain. This is then documented repeatedly and independently by *"Miners"* across the globe attempting to *"Hash"* these transaction and *"Time Stamp"* them first (with atomic clocks, no less) so that they will be rewarded with a part of the fees. Maybe it sounds like *"Sci-Fi"* but we are here, now. (Many, many other books here if you want the deep dive, but not completely germane to your *"Pursuit of Ownership"* other than *"It Works and is Safe"*. You want to know *"What time it is"* not *"How to build a watch"* and this book will not make the mistake so many others do. If you appreciate this approach, please tell your friend about this book).

As an important added bonus, this process thereby solves the *"Double Pay"* issue where you cannot spend the same, unique coin, twice. The system is essentially a *"Truth Machine"* without human intervention, as long as *"Time"* keeps marching forward (deep baby, I know).

Now let's revisit what the *"Seven Advantages"* of great currency, and see how Bitcoin compares:

1. <u>Divisibility</u> – A Bitcoin can be broken into 1,000,000 "Satoshi" (So you can buy any part of a Bitcoin and spend it similarly).
2. <u>Store of Value</u> – Limited quantity forever and *"Appreciating"*.
3. <u>Durability</u> – Immutable due to encryption.
4. <u>Uniformity</u> – All 21,000,000 of them.
5. <u>Transportability</u> – Frictionless transfers across the globe safely.
6. <u>Consensus of Acceptance</u> – Growing with *"S-Curve adoption"* as all new technologies do.
7. <u>Non-Counterfeitablity</u> – Versus our paper fiat currencies, hilarious!

Although there are so many benefits (including the most efficient and cost effective way to send money on the planet, as just a small one), until the infrastructure is built out, and adoption increases, there are manageable risks. First, the Bitcoin is volatile and can swing with large percentage changes in a day. Over time this should abate but for now, we are all in the *"Wild West"* to a certain extent. As the Venture Capitalists often say, *"When the roads are paved, you can drive your Cadillac up, and then toss the valet your keys; The opportunity is over"*. Holding Bitcoins over time has proved to be a productive and lucrative strategy.

When humanity is introduced to new technology, there is a very predictable **"S-Curve"** of adoption (sometimes also called a *"Bell Curve of Adoption"*). Similar to cell phones, few people at first *("Innovators and Early Adopters")* have them, then cell phones catch on, and the curve goes up quickly. The last stage is *"Late Adopters"* which finally get converted. Imagine this pattern as an "S" that you draw from the bottom upwards. See:

http://en.wiipedia.org/wiki/Technology_Adoption_Life_Cycle

for a through overview. At time of press, we are leaving the *"Innovator Stage"* and entering the *"Early Adopter Stage"* which is a wonderful thing if you are reading this book. As you look at the percentage of adoption and the percentage to go, you begin to see where the $250,000 to $1,000,000+ value per Bitcoin predictions come from, with approximately $150 trillion in world currency! Yeah us!

6 A NEW ASSET CLASS

"Things Done Changed"
-   The Notorious B.I.G.

A new *"Asset Class"*, why not just Gold and Silver you ask? Great question and let's delve into the reality of this proposition. Gold, Silver, and Bitcoin are mined and thereby are scarce (Gold and Silver with picks and axes, Bitcoin with electricity). Gold, Silver, and Bitcoin all have intrinsic value and are all readily tradeable for Fiat Currency (Gold and Silver's prices are manipulated, but much has already been written about that). Where they begin to differ is security. With Gold and Silver you will need a security guard and an armored truck, but not with Bitcoin if done correctly. Would you break off a little Gold or Silver and send it to a creditor via the mail or courier?   With Bitcoin it can be sent at light speed, and very safely due to encryption, even if the vendor does not take Bitcoin. Yes, there are now *"Crypto/Fiat Debit Cards"* that convert crypto to fiat with a swipe of a card (yes, on credit card terminals) behind the scenes without the merchant seeing any difference (They debit your crypto currency, convert to Fiat automatically, and send Fiat to the merchant/creditor directly)! Don't even get me started on how we would send Gold or Silver to another country.

Wealth is pouring into this new *"Asset Class"* from across the globe, and believe it or not, until now, Wall Street has missed this one. They are quickly getting up to speed due to client demand and there will be a tremendous amount of money pouring in, as they establish these direct channels. Furthermore, through educational offerings like this book (Tell you friends, please, my kids are hungry), more and more people are understanding and seeing the road to ownership. Remember there are a limited number of coins and an avalanche of wealth jamming in, so the price will continue to rise as long as this trend continues. Like a cakewalk or musical chairs, there are only so many chairs to sit in. But unlike these games, you can sit down early and stay. I like this game already! If you are reading this book then you know the music has started to play, get a seat my brothers and sisters, and just sit down to win the game!

7 REGULATION AND TAXATION

Again, I am not an investment advisor, or a C.P.A., or a Tax Attorney so please consult your entire professional team before making any decisions on cryptocurrency.

Currently, Bitcoin is not regulated by a government agency in the United States.   Regulation is coming and will be a great thing for the *"Cryptocurrency"*, this will further legitimize and give definitive guidance to, law abiding citizens like us. It has already been recognized as legal tender in Japan and Switzerland, and will most likely start its Regulation journey in the Far East. China and Russia will come out with further Regulations and direction in the coming year and then, will be followed by similar guardrails in Western Countries including the U.S. Most likely this will be Regulation in the area of *"ICOs or Initial Coin Offerings"* (More on this in a future book, stay tuned) and further *"Exchange"* limitations and *"Capital Requirements"*. All of these things will further legitimize Bitcoin.

As for taxes, PAY THEM. After all, someone once said, *"Give Caesar what is Caesar's".* Essentially if you hold Bitcoin for less than a year, you are taxed at *"Ordinary Income Rates"* and if you hold them for over 12 months you will receive *"Capital Gains Treatment".* There is a bill in Congress that would allow you to pay no tax on purchases less than $687. This would help us, as we spend these *"Cryptocurrency"* for day-to-day items. Currently, every transaction after the initial conversion from Fiat is a *"Taxable Event"* that you will need to self-report to your taxing authorities. *"Crypto/Fiat Debit Cards"* will help with this accounting. Consult your professional advisors as laws will change quickly, and much more Regulation will present itself, as time passes.

8 MYTHS AND URBAN LEGENDS

"Don't Call it a Come Back"
- LL Cool J

Bitcoin Is In A Bubble – Do a quick search on the Internet about Bitcoin being in a *"Bubble"*, and then see when the article was written and what price Bitcoin traded at then. Bitcoin hit a new high today, so everyone who ever invested in and held on, has made money. There are a limited number of Bitcoins and wealth is dramatically pouring into them. This means that Bitcoins will keep experiencing price appreciation until that stops, and that will not be soon. In a future chapter, I will show you where you can check the inflow of *"Fiat Currency to Bitcoin"* for free. Lastly remember, Bitcoin was in a *"Bubble"* at *"Parity"* with the US Dollar ($1.00), then *"Parity"* with Gold, and again at $10,000. Next stop $100,000, impossible, right!? The Media needs to get over it, you are and have been wrong, admit it and move on.

Bitcoin Will Be Hacked – No, the software *is "Open Source"* so it is out there to be seen, readily, and has been since inception. It has never been hacked and someone who says this, does not know what they are taking about (Again, plenty of other great *"Coding"* books here – Apparently there are even more people, purporting to be experts, who have not read them).

"They" Will Turn Off The Internet – I would always suggest having some *"Walking Around Money"* in *"Fiat Currency"* for now in case the battery dies on your phone. *"They"* are not going to turn off the Internet. Think of how businesses, economies, and the globe is now dependent upon the Internet to survive, literally. Besides if it ever was, which it won't, than, when it came back up, all of the decentralized information would be, again, available on the *"Blockchain"*. So it would have to stay off forever (See Turkey's reaction to *"Turning Off the Internet"*). Remember the US government invented the Internet to communicate during a nuclear war for gosh sakes.

The Federal Reserve, Governments, And Banks Will Not Allow Bitcoin to Grow – To late, it is already out there and they cannot get it out of the Internet, as it is software. As governments have attempted to control Bitcoin (See China's attempt at Bitcoin $4,000), the attempts have only fueled further growth of Bitcoin. More importantly, there will be unprecedented GDP growth for countries that embrace it, and build business around it. You really believe that the U.S., Russia, Europe, China, or the rest of Asia want to miss out on that (See *"Prisoners Dilemma"*)?

Only Criminals, Drug Dealers, and Terrorists Use Bitcoin – Bitcoin is *"Traceable"* and, as a result, criminals are using other privacy *"Cryptocurrencies"* to hide their tracks like Monero, etc. (More on that in a future book). Given the cost effectiveness and the efficiencies, for legitimate, real world applications Bitcoin will provide honest commerce a wonderful alternative/new solution. By the way, the US Dollar in cash has been a much bigger offender historically, for these elements of society, and IS actually untraceable. *Just sayin'.*

Anonymity – As discussed above, Bitcoin can be tracked from the first time you convert Fiat on an Exchange, to where you send it from, to where you send it to, and then onward. As law abiding citizens, this is not an issue but this myth is out there.

No Place Accepts Bitcoin Currently – Maybe not everywhere yet, but with a *"Crypto/Fiat Debit Card"* most places do. Much more infrastructure is being worked on, and it will become easier and easier over time. Wait until Coinbase comes out with a *"Crypto Debit Card"* that uses *"Cryptocurrency"* directly on their own *"Network"* (More on that in future Chapters).

Bitcoin Is Too Volatile To Buy a Daily Cup of Coffee For The Same Price – Yes, now, but that has been part of its incredible upward trend. Over time this has been an *"Appreciating Currency"* which sounds awesome to me! As long as wealth keeps pouring in, it will rise, and then eventually stabilize at much higher values. Effectively, your coffee keeps getting cheaper; Darn I hate when that happens.

<u>Bitcoin is a Ponzi or a Pyramid Scheme</u> – It is not either. No one is paying you out to get in, and no one is working underneath or above you. You are *"Storing Wealth"* in a limited commodity, that has global value, because of its utilizable characteristics. It is that simple, just like Gold.

<u>Bitcoin is the *"Tulip Bubble"* All Over Again</u> – Tulips did not have a business case to disintermediate an industry or, in this case, the global currency market….yes, it is an industry. This one really needs to stop, it is just plain stupid and painful. Most of the *"Tulip Bubble"* was actually caused by the *"Debasing of the "Florin""* *(Formerly the European Reserve Currency)* by removing Gold as a result of *"Accommodative Government Policymaking"*. People misguidedly rushed into *"Tulips"* as a *"Store of Value"*. Holy Moly, exactly what not to do, keeps getting clearer to me. You will never hear this when *"Media Pundits"* speak of the *"Tulip Mania"* but, do the research, and become enlightened.

<u>Bitcoin is Not Elastic So It Will Fail</u> – Neither is Gold technically, and it has stood the test of time, for 5,000+ years. By the way, look where elastic has gotten us, and history to…next myth please!

<u>Bitcoin Cannot Continue Like This</u> – It can and it will. Again, a limited number, wealth pouring in, and only 1 to 2% adoption, thus far. On a *"Log Scale"*, which is how new technology gets adopted, the graph looks tame and predictable. Go to: http://coinmarketcap.com and double click on the Bitcoin Icon. Go to the Bitcoin Chart and see the *"Scary "Linear Chart""* that the Media always touts as, *"Tulip Mania II, The Sequel"*. Now click the button below the chart for *"Log Scale"*. This is the real chart we should be looking at for a *"Bubble"* and, of course, we look good to date. Do you remember the old shampoo commercial about telling two friends and then they tell two friends….this is how technology (or in the commercial, shampoo) is adopted and this is why we view it on a *"Log Scale"*. It can continue like this and it will continue like this for the foreseeable future, with or without you…

<u>Bitcoin is Too Abstract, I Will Never Get Comfortable And Invest</u> – You already understand it, and are already using many similar items, the difference is that they were given to you and, as such, you were ok not touching them. Have you ever taken a free flight with miles? Have you ever got something for free with credit card points? You already understand the concept, because I am sure you have never held an airline mile or credit card point in your hand! On the flip side, I am sure that you know that they both have value. The difference now is that you will have to purchase this value and, wait for it, it can appreciate while you own!

Bitcoin will not be telling you that it is now, *"More Miles for a Same Free Flight, Please"*, but I bet the airlines have.

9 F.U.D. VS. F.O.M.O.

"With All This Money That We Can Make, Why Y'all Cats Wanna Playa Hate "

- Mase

Ah, humanities' favorite motivator – F.U.D. or Fear, Uncertainty, and Doubt. Since the dawn of humanity, humans have been using these three strategies to get other humans to do what they want them to. It is early in the adoption cycle, and without fail, all of these will be used by Governments, Central Banks, and Wall Street, as they see the possibility of power being decentralized and given back to the people. Can you blame them, we have already seen what *"Disintermediation"* does to industries and power structures. Their lives will irreparably and drastically be changed as adoption accelerates. Do not be surprised, if coordinated F.U.D. campaigns, are uncovered as Bitcoin grows. Really, they are only attempting to slow adoption so they can get a piece of the pie for themselves, or so that the economy has time to transition. They ALL know that Bitcoin is here to stay. As it has been since the dawn of humanity, we mock what we do not understand. This will be Governments', Banks', and the Media's FAVORITE TACTIC. Look for this *'Tell'*. Watch the Media discredit this book for using these great artists' words, at the beginning of each chapter (We do not precede legitimate economic discussions with quotes such as these, or something even dumber). You read it here, before it happen in the *"Mainstream Financial Media"*, or in an *"Online Review"*. They always mock what they do not understand. This does not make the truth less true, does it?

Placing a close second for human motivation, will be – F.O.M.O or Fear Of Missing Out. Generally, when people first become aware of Bitcoin, they go through the *'I Missed Out, Phase''* and then, over time, as they see that they actually, did not. They then get educated, and begin to experience F.O.M.O., until it just gets to be too much, and they finally adopt.

Next, Bitcoin goes up in value, and, in time, they start speaking in terms of F.O.M.O. with friends and family, encouraging them to begin to utilize this new, game-changing, technology. We want more people to interact with us inside this new technology to show them we are right, if nothing else. Didn't we all just do this with cell phones and tablets?

10 HOW AND WHERE TO BUY

"And If You Don't Know, Now You Know, You Know…"
- The Notorious B.I.G.

First, you will need cash, a debit card, a credit card, or most likely a checking account that is above $0. Most of us do not have a tremendous amount but, we have some combination of the above. This is great, because I suggest starting with *"Nickels and Dimes"* which means starting with smaller amounts to get an understanding of how to buy, in the way or ways, that most suit your personal situation. I would only use a credit card if you already have the money to pay it off immediately and I would never risk money that you cannot afford lose.

There are predominately two ways to purchase Bitcoin. The first, is a Bitcoin ATM which will accept Fiat cash. The fees are steep, and you will have to locate an ATM but, if it the only way you can obtain, then it is better than sitting on the sidelines. The second and more traditional way to purchase Bitcoin, is through the *"Exchanges"*. Some will take Fiat Currency (not all do), and they will ask you to utilize a credit card, to link to a bank account for an ACH transfer, or will allow you to wire money in from your financial institution.

The two major Exchanges in the US that will take Fiat, US dollars, are the Coinbase Exchange and the Gemini Exchange. Coinbase is out of San Francisco and is the largest Exchange in the US, it can be accessed at http://coinbase.com. Gemini is based in New York and can be accessed at http://gemini.com. Both of these, to date, have never been hacked, have very good security, and are highly rated by their users.

The government has mandated that they *"KYU"* or Know Your Users so, the sign up process can be a little arduous and you will need to be PERSISTENT (4 out of 5 that attempt to buy, quit before finished, but NOT you, you have this book). They will ask for pictures of both sides of your Drivers License, a recent selphie, a recent utility bill, possibly a Social Security Card, and then they may ask you to take a picture through their own app to verify it is you. You may as well digitizes these things (take picture and send to computer) now to be ahead of the game. Then, they will ask you to do a *"Two Factor Identification"* which means that you will be asked for your phone number and they will send you a code to insure it is you. After all this, you may get an email back stating that something was rejected, they could not accept it as proof of ID, or that it was too blurry, it had too many pixels in the photo, etc. Be PERSISTENT and think of it as a challenge. Coinbase for example has been opening 40,000 to 300,000 accounts a day! At the time of press, this is the #1 Downloaded App, per day, on the globe.

Post account setup, you will need to link a debit/credit card, link a bank account, or wire in money. When you link a debit/credit card (input card number, expiration, CID number), they will charge your account two small amounts, say $1.17 and $1.97. You will need to go into your card account and see these two charges, and then input the cents part of the charge, to validate the payment method (they will then credit these back). Allegedly, you are now able to buy Bitcoin or transfer US dollars in this amount to your *"Exchange Account"*. Very frequently, when you try to transfer money from your Bank or Credit Provider, the Bank will *"Detect Fraud"* and cancel the transaction. Simply pick up the phone and ask them to allow the next attempt. If I was paranoid, I would think that the banks do not like to see Fiat Currency flow to the Exchanges but, they gave me a free toaster, so that just cannot be true.

The process for setting up a checking or savings account is similar. The will either ask for the *"Routing Number"* and *"Account Number"* or they will ask you to pick your bank from a list and then literally login with you bank Username and Password. From there you will be asked to click on the Account you would like to *"Link"*. Again be ready for delays, fraud alerts, and calls to your bank but be PERSISTENT and you will get there. Generally, the Exchanges will let you spend more money with ACHs versus credit/debit cards. On both Exchanges with these links established, the Exchange will let you lock into a price today while the funds clear.

The process for *"Wiring In"* is detailed on each Exchange, including what bank and what code you need to put on to on the wire itself. This will take a trip to the bank and a lot of nosey questions from your Bank Manager about what you are doing *"YOUR"* the money, to which you reply that you are sending it to an investment account (do not be surprised if they try to sell you their financial products, politely say no thank you unless you want 00.5% return). Coinbase sometimes sends these wires back if they are not perfect, in their eyes, and there is nobody on a phone to talk to. Gemini actually lets you detail in your account what you will be wiring. They then send you an email with all the information that you can take directly to your banker. Technically, there is not a limit as to what you can send, and funds are usually available that same day.

Once you are *"Linked"*, or have money in your Coinbase Account, you point and click to purchase, in the *"Buy/Sell"* Tab, fill out the desired amount, and another click to *"Confirm"*, you are an owner. In Gemini, you first put US Dollars into your Account, and then you can buy Bitcoin directly on the *"Platform"*. Both Exchanges have video tutorials on their sites, which I strongly recommend viewing a couple of times, before executing a transaction.

You have signed up, proven you are you, linked your Fiat Account, transferred money, and bought your first Bitcoin. Thank you for your PERSISTENCE, and congratulation!

11 NOW WHAT?

*"Chill, I Got My Umbrella........Chumpy,
I break Up With Him Before He Dump Me"
-    Missy Elliot, Timberland, and Ann Peebles*

So am I done? Unfortunately no, but you are inside the *"Bitcoin World"* on an Exchange. The problem with Exchanges is that they could be hacked at some point (See *"Mt. Gox"* in search engine query – Exchange that was hacked and people lost money), and you do not have your *"Private Keys"* in your possession (Similar to having cash in your wallet versus in the custody of the bank). *"Private Keys"* are a long series of 26-35 numbers and letters which may be capitalized or not, and this matters (Example: **1BvBMSEYstWetqTFn5Au4m4GFg7xJaNVN2** - welcome to crypto world). They change every time Bitcoin is sent on the *"Blockchain"* - The cryptographic, distributed ledger, that powers Bitcoin (Whew!). Since, Bitcoin is *"Unregulated"* and there is no FDIC protection for Bitcoin, if it is stolen, it is gone (Time for *"Personal Responsibility"* once again, all things come full circle, eventually). Never share your "Private Keys" with anyone, ever. Ok, but where do I send it, you ask? You will be sending it to your Wallet but this is a *"Digital Wallet"* either online, on your computer, on paper, or offline, in what is called *"Cold Storage"*.

12 WHERE TO STORE

"They Took My Rings, They Took My Rolex,
I looked at the Brother, Said "Damn, What's Next?""
-   Warren G and Nate Dogg

Ummm, I cannot touch it so where do I put it, or something like that, I think? You are not alone in this question and there is a great answer, but it involves *"Personal Responsibility"*...there are those darn words again. Remember, Bitcoin is *"Unregulated"* and not currently backed by the FDIC, or anyone else for that matter. If you lose them, like cash, they are gone. If your *"Wallet"* is hacked (Bitcoin itself has never been hacked) and someone gets your Bitcoins, they are gone, just like cash. As a result of these stark truths, choose your wallets wisely and then protect them.

Essentially there are 7 basic *"Wallet Strategies"* or *"Wallet Types"*:

First, there are the Exchanges where you bought these Bitcoins. With Stocks and Bonds this has historically been fine, but with Bitcoin there are too many folks trying to get at these with computer skills far in access of most of us. I would not store them here for any length of time, or in any great amount. I would *"Send Out"* upon receiving the Bitcoins. (More on this to come).

Second, Coinbase has added a *"Vault"* option which has some promise but still makes most nervous. Essentially you have to call out your Bitcoins, and then for two days you get emails confirming you want this to happen. After those two days, without you canceling, they are available.

Third, there are various types of *"Online Wallets"* where you send websites your Bitcoins and they protect them for you. Effectively they are in the cloud and not on your computer or other device. Again this is too scary for most, and you do not possess your *"Private Keys"*.

Fourth, there are *"Mobile Wallets"* that are, of course, on your cell phone. Although these will eventually be a great place to have small amounts of cryptocurrency for purchases, directly or through 3rd party apps, we can do better.

Fifth, there are *"Computer Wallets"* which are pretty good because you have your own *"Private Keys"*, but hackers can try to access your computer anytime it is online or via viruses, spearfishing, etc.

Sixth, there are *"Paper Wallets"* which are essentially a print out of your *"Private Keys"* that can be stored in a safe, or cut into two pieces and give to two separate people to safely store. If you go this route, choose people that you really trust because without the entire *"Private Key"*, the Bitcoins are as good as lost.

Seventh and finally, there are *"Cold Storage Wallets"* which are almost universally agreed upon, to be the best for security. These started as USB drives that had the *"Private Keys"* stored on them. Now they have morphed into a dedicated device with 2 separate microchips in them. These devices, like the Ledger and Trezor, keep your *"Private Keys"* on one chip and the other chip is used to interface with the encrypted platform software online. Your keys are kept offline always, until you need them. Nice!

13 HOW TO STORE SECURELY AND CHILL

"Get Up, Get Get, Get Down…
911 is a Joke in Yo' Town"
 - *Flavor Flav with Public Enemy*

The strongest suggestion to you, by the Community, is to *"Store"* Bitcoins in a *"Cold Storage Wallet"* as it is believed to be the most secure. Let's take the *"Ledger Blue"* for example (many others are very good and operate similarly, but, just for illustrative purposes to begin understand the basics). A large variety of choices and price points are available from online retailers.

When your Ledger Blue arrives, you will unpack it and power it up. You will need to connect the USB provided to a computer to charge the unit. Additionally, you will need to go to: http://ledgerwallet.com to download the *"Ledger Manager"* and *"Bitcoin App"* directly from the site. It is recommended to do this on Google Chrome, due to its cryptographic secure web page capabilities. You will then have these apps in the *"Apps Section of Google Chrome"* when you pull up this Browser, always. On the Leger website, there are simple videos to walk you through each step of set-up, including your *"20 Word Recovery Password"* and your *"Daily Password"*.

After you have accomplished this, I would memorize your "Daily Password" as you only get 3 attempts before the device locks down, and I would store, in an actual safe or safety deposit box, your *"20 Word Recovery Password"*.

What happens if my Ledger Blue is lost or stolen, you ask? Fortunately, you can just order another one, imprint your *"20 Word Recovery Password"*, then sync with the Internet app (There is a video on the website for this too) and, presto, you are back in business. Fairly, slick many say!

Lastly, now you have bought Bitcoin on Coinbase, and are ready to *"Send Out"* to your Ledger Blue wallet. Go to the *"Accounts Tab"* on Coinbase and push the *"Send Button"* under the BTC Wallet at the top of the page. Best to do this with 2 separate computer screens running at same time, if at all possible. If not open two browser on the same computer.

Now hook your Ledger Blue to the USB Cable that is connected to your computer. Go to you Google Chrome Apps and single click the Bitcoin App. This will take a moment to come up, and you are in.

Once in, hit the "Receive Button" which will generate a *"Public Key"* (A place to send Bitcoins that does not impact your *"Private Keys"*, in any way). Please highlight the entire *"Public Key"* and then with the *"Copy"* function on your computer, and copy it into the Coinbase *"Send To"* box. It will then ask you how much to *"Send Out"*, and you type in your amount desired, or hit *"Max Amount"*, if you want to send it all at once. Check the *"Public Key Address"* in your Ledger Blue App to the one in the Coinbase website, and when you are SURE they match, press *"Send"*. CoinBase will take you through another screen to confirm (check again here because if it is sent to the wrong *"Public Address"*, it is gone forever) and may ask for a *"Two Factor Authentication"* (many videos about this are posted on Coinbase for free) then press the *"Confirm Button"* and it is sent.

Now, look at your Ledger Blue Wallet App and wait 10 minutes (sometimes much longer depending on *"Network Traffic"*) and it will appear like an email does. First, it will appear as *"Unconfirmed"* and as miners hash it, it will eventually be *"Confirmed"* and in your Ledger Blue. Unplug your Ledger Blue and now your Bitcoin is in *"Cold Storage"* and off the Internet, congratulations! Now, chill.

This is where you begin to see why Bankers do not like Bitcoin, because it was so much easier (after you know the process, of course) and much cheaper, to send money to anywhere in the world. Again, I always recommend buying and sending *"Nickels and Dimes"* or small amounts until this is all second nature which, will happen sooner than you think. Please re-read this chapter a couple of times before attempting any of this and make sure to see the videos on Coinbase for a visual walk through a couple of times.

14 MONITORING

"I Can't Believe, Today was a Good Day..."
-   Ice Cube

There are so many great places to glean, cutting edge information in the cryptoshere, and the following are just a few to get you started:

Market Prices of Cryptocurrency
- https://WorldCoinIndex.com
- https://CoinMarketCap.com

Charting
- https://tradeview.com
- http://Gdax.com

News Articles
- https://cointelegraph.com
- https://BitcoinMagazine.com

Direct
- Twitter
    1. Bitcoin
    2. SGTreport
    3. CME Group
    4. Bitcoin Foundation
    5. Hacked.com

15 HODL

"In the Land of the Blind, the One-Eyed Man is King"
- Erasmus

Most people get to a point where even a 50% pull back is above their entry point but, the volatility is for real. You will *"White Knuckle It"* on your first pull back for sure, but HODL or *"Hold On For Dear Life"* (See Reddit for the original article)! Recently, the pullbacks have been less severe and the recovery time is accelerating but, that will not last forever. Be ready to turn off your computer if you have to and just HODL. Remember where we are on the S-Curve from an adoption perspective, and we are early baby!

Every time you watch Bitcoin hit a new high realize that everyone that has purchased and held, to that point, is *"Above Water"* and many, many more are really doing well! Look at Apple's Stock and look way back to a time when people thought it was a scary time for the Company. Now, that pullback is just a blip, and those that held on were treated very well.

Although there is no guarantee, traders have not done as well after-tax, as the HODLers. Furthermore, what a great and achievable strategy, that will not require you to sit in front of a computer screen all day. Cast your gaze out on a longer time horizon, and know where your *"Exit Points"* will be, if any. Even better, know what you will do with those funds in the real world.

Remember that *"In the Land of the Blind, the One-Eyed Man is King"*…use your *"Eye"* (from this book) to see the opportunity that others do not!

16 WHAT IS NEXT

"It Feels Good Puttin' Money in Your Mailbox...
...You are Appreciated"
- 2 Pac

If you eventually decide that Bitcoin, post due diligence and consultation with your financial team, is for you, it is important to always remember that Bitcoin is *"Speculative"*. Never risk more than you can comfortably lose.

If you are fortunate, and this trend continues remember that *"It is Just Money"* and that life has much higher priorities – Faith, Family, Others Less Fortunate, Country, Etc.. While I understand that BOTH, *"Money Cannot Buy You Happiness"* and that *"Although it Can't, It Sure Can Take the Edge Off of Misery"*, you are so much more than your net worth.

I encourage you to think now of what good you can do with an increase in net worth, and where you would like to spend more of your time in life. Many pundits are saying that *"This is the Opportunity of Our Lifetimes"* but what good is it if we have no real plan, and it works out? Really spend some time thinking about this too, during your *"Personal Due Diligence Period"* post reading this book.

Ok, off my soapbox…until our next book.

17 THE FUTURE

"Will It Ever Stop, Yo I Don't Know "
- Vanilla Ice

The future for Bitcoin is uncertain, as the future always is, but this is an *"Asset Class"* that is here to stay. Could Bitcoin be *"Dethroned"* as the *"Reserve Cryptocurrency"*, of course, but not likely in the immediate future.

My belief, along with many others, is that it ultimately becomes what *"Wires"* at banks are today. It will be primarily used to buy a house or a car or by businesses to settle transactions, nationally and internationally. If this is the case, then HODLing will be a *"Good Day"* for those that are disciplined.

What price will it stabilize at, you ask? There are so many predictions out there but as long as money is going in, it will continue to climb. Most likely it will reach $100,000 to several million if its current trajectory continues, but no one really knows. Up, is always a good answer at a cocktail party but, we will be ready for many large crashes along the way (Look at Amazon, these crashes are inconsequential to long term holders now, and Bitcoin will most likely be the same way).

The only place I know of that has had a 100% rate of success for predictions is (Some are still to come to fruition – like *"A Quart of Wheat and Three Quarts of Barley Were Each Valued at "One Denarius"*), the Bible. Sorry, if in our PC World that offends any, just check it out if you are willing to do the research, and can maintain an open-mind. The last Chapter is a scary one and also talks about someone or something eventually taking control of all money, globally. I do not believe that we are there yet, but stay vigilant as future events unfold for humanity (Topic for yet another Book, I suppose). As they say, *"The Truth Will Set You Free, But First It Will Probably, Piss You Off"*!

Thank you for reading and *"listening"* to me, as my wife has literally *"HAD IT"* with this stuff! Please remember, if you liked this book, tell your friends and family about it, as *"My kids are hungry"*...

Cheers until next time,

James

ABOUT THE PUBLISHERS

One Concept Media was formed to address cutting edge technologies in an approachable and easy to read format. Our books are meant to aggregate disparate knowledge on emerging topics in a conceptual framework that holistically introduces you to the concept. We strive to deliver *"One Sitting Reads"* that can be enjoyed in a coffee shop, on a flight, during an early morning alone, etc. We believe that if a book is too detailed and laborious, it becomes useless to the reader, as many times, they do not finish it.

Specifically, this book is a starting point and for informational purposes only. One Concept Media and Bitcoin Wealth are Educational Publishing Houses not investment advisors, tax attorneys, or CPAs and their books are not meant as investment advice. The purpose of this book is only to get you familiar with the concepts surrounding Bitcoin and guide you to some other places to begin your personal due diligence. Before making any investments you should consult your investment advisor, tax attorney, and CPA. If you do not understand this please go back and read again. Thank you in advance.

www.OneMediaConcept.com

www.BitcoinWealth.com